THE
PYRAMID
POEMS OF MASONS:
SYMBOLS AND TOOLS OF THE CRAFT
CONSTRUCTED BY DAVID EASTON POTTS

David Easton Potts

Published by Broken Column Press
Illustrations by Bro. Jonathan Heisey-Grove of Heisey-Grove Design
ISBN: 978-0-9861495-2-8

IN
THESE VERSES
ARE NO MASONIC
SECRETS, ONLY TRUTHS WRITTEN
TO REVEAL WHAT'S IN OUR HEARTS AND MINDS

PREFACE

The Pyramid Poems are inspired by and derived from the York Rite degrees as conferred in Virginia - Entered Apprentice through Royal Arch. Masons from other jurisdictions will note the inclusion of the Select and Royal Masters Cryptic degrees. These have been part of the Grand Council of Royal Arch Masons in Virginia since 1841. At that time their order was reversed to better suit their inclusion in the Virginia Blue Lodge and Royal Arch degrees.

The degree sections in this book are in conferral order to honor our traditions. In chronological order according to the events they portray, however, they would be Entered Apprentice, Fellowcraft, Mark Master, Select Master, Royal Master, Master Mason, Most Excellent Master, and Royal Arch Degrees. Not included in this publication is the Past Master degree, exemplified to maintain an ancient custom requiring all Royal Arch Masons to have previously served as Master in the East, although some of the Old Charges from that degree are in the "What Came Before" section. Also not included is the Super Excellent Master degree, which in Virginia is an honorary degree conferred at Grand Chapter convocations. If positioned in the chronological lineup it would be between the Most Excellent Master and Royal Arch Degrees.

The chivalric orders of the Commandery of Knights Templar of Virginia are also missing from this collection. Although they are an essential part of our York Rite, indeed they are the culmination of York Rite Masonry in the United States, the orders take us in a different direction. And what a wonderful and fulfilling direction that is and what a rich tradition of two hundred years of Knights Templary we have in Virginia.

I agree with Virginia's John Dove (1792-1896) who wrote in his *Royal Arch Textbook*, "This degree is indescribably more august, sublime, and important than all which precede it; and is the summit and perfection of ancient Masonry." And I'm aligned with English author and Freemason W. L. Wilmshurst (1867-1939). He came to understand from his studies of ancient mystics and philosophers that the Royal Arch is the greatest and most meaningful degree in Masonry: the exalted ending of a physical and spiritual journey from ordinary man to something more enlightened, more perfect, more divine. And that is why this collection of poems is arranged the way it is.

I owe special thanks to Episcopal Priest Worshipful Brother Gordon Bardos who opened the door in Vermont many years ago when I knocked the first time and Right Worshipful Brother Carl Weaver who opened the door in Virginia when I knocked the second time.

So many Brothers and Companions have enlightened (and counseled) me in Masonry over the years that they cannot all be listed. You know who you are. You will be in my heart and mind as long as I live and breathe. And perhaps after that.

While inspired by York Rite printed materials, this poetic creation is neither an official publication of the Grand Lodge of Ancient Free and Accepted Masons of Virginia nor the Grand Chapter of Royal Arch Masons in Virginia. Any misrepresentations are strictly my own.

PROLOGUE

THESE
POEMS OF
YORK RITE MASONRY
ARE OF THE OLD DOMINION:
ENTERED APPRENTICE THROUGH ROYAL ARCH

FIVE
LINES OF ODD
NUMBERS IN VERSES -
ONE THREE FIVE SEVEN AND NINE
SYLLABLES - TWENTY-FIVE AND NO MORE

EACH
PYRAMID
POEM STANDS ALONE,
AND JOINS IN SEQUENCE TO SHINE
LIGHT ON THE ANCIENT YORK RITE DEGREES

WHAT CAME BEFORE

WHEN
DURING THE
REIGN OF ATHELSTANE,
HIS WISE BROTHER PRINCE EDWIN
RECEIVED A CHARTER FOR FREEMASONS

TO
HOLD YEARLY
ASSEMBLIES IN YORK.
EDWIN THEN SUMMONED THEM ALL
TO MEET WITH HIM IN CONGREGATION

AND
REQUIRED THEM
TO FIND AND BRING THE
ANCIENT WRITINGS TO FRAME THE
CONSTITUTIONS OF ENGLISH LODGES

OH
SOLOMON,
MY SON, FORGET NOT
MY LAW AND REMOVE NOT THE
ANCIENT LANDMARK MY FATHERS HAVE SET

DO
NOT TRANSGRESS
THE OLD LANDMARKS NOR
IN ANY WAY VIOLATE
MASONRY'S GENIUS AND SOUL

THUS
THE ANCIENT
MASONIC LANDMARKS
ENTRUSTED TO YOUR CHARGE YOU
ARE TO CAREFULLY PRESERVE AND KEEP

THE
BASIC LAW
OF OUR NOBLE CRAFT
RESTS ON THE OLD CHARGES AND
THE CONSTITUTIONS OF MASONRY

YOU
AGREE TO
BE A GOOD MAN AND
TRUE AND STRICTLY OBEY THE
MORAL LAWS OF THE FRATERNITY

YOU
AGREE TO
CONFORM TO THE LAWS
OF THE COUNTRY IN WHICH YOU
LIVE AND BE A PEACEFUL CITIZEN

YOU
PROMISE NOT
TO BE CONCERNED WITH
PLOTS AND CONSPIRACIES BUT
PATIENTLY WAIT FOR LEGISLATION

YOU
AGREE TO
PAY APPROPRIATE
RESPECT TO THE MAGISTRATES
AND ACT HONORABLY BY ALL MEN

YOU
AGREE TO
AVOID PRIVATE PIQUES
AND QUARRELS AND ALSO GUARD
AGAINST INTEMPERANCE AND EXCESS

YOU
AGREE TO
BE CAUTIOUS IN YOUR
CARRIAGE AND BEHAVIOR AND
COURTEOUS ALL TIMES TO YOUR BRETHREN

YOU
PROMISE TO
RESPECT GENUINE
BRETHREN AND DISCOUNTENANCE
ALL THE IMPOSTERS AND DISSENTERS

YOU
AGREE TO
PROMOTE THE COMMON
GOOD OF SOCIETY AND
TO CULTIVATE ALL SOCIAL VIRTUES

David Easton Potts

ENTERED APPRENTICE

ENTERED APPRENTICE DEGREE

THE
MAN SEEKS, THEN
KNOCKS AT THE DOOR, AND
IF HE BE GOOD AND KEEN, THE
MASTER AND BROTHERS WILL ACCEPT HIM

GRANT
OH FATHER
THAT THIS CANDIDATE
BECOMES A TRUE AND FAITHFUL
BROTHER UNTIL THE END OF OUR DAYS

HOW
GOOD IT IS
TO SEE THE BRETHREN
DWELLING TOGETHER AS ONE,
AS DEW DESCENDED UPON ZION

EIGHT
HOURS DIVIDE
A FREEMASON'S DAY:
EIGHT SERVICING GOD AND MAN,
EIGHT FOR VOCATIONS, AND EIGHT FOR REST

A
GAVEL FOR
BREAKING ROUGH ROCKS, WITH
NOBLE AND GLORIOUS USE
OF FITTING OUR MINDS AS LIVING STONES

BADGE
AND EMBLEM
OF INNOCENCE AND
HONOR, THE LAMB SKIN APRON
IS CONFERRED WITHOUT SPOT OR BLEMISH

FOR
WISDOM TO
BUILD, STRENGTH TO SUPPORT,
AND BEAUTY TO ADORN, ALL
GREAT AND IMPORTANT UNDERTAKINGS

HIGH
ABOVE ARE
STARRY DECKED HEAVENS,
WHERE ALL GOOD MASONS HOPE TO
ARRIVE WITH AID OF FAITH AND LADDER

ON
THE ALTAR
LAYS THE HOLY BOOK
WITH THE SQUARE OF THE MASTER
AND COMPASSES FOR THE ABLE CRAFT

THREE
ALTAR LIGHTS,
SMALL AGAINST THE DARK,
GLOW BRIGHT ENOUGH TO REVEAL
THE OLD AWE IN WHAT WE SENSE AND FEEL

FOUR
HARD CORNERS
OF THE LIGHTED SQUARE,
CIRCUMAMBULATE-SOFTENED,
GIVE PLACE TO HEAL A BROTHER'S NATURE

FROM
EAST TO WEST,
BETWEEN NORTH AND SOUTH,
FREEMASONRY EXTENDS, AND
IN EVERY CLIME A MASON IS FOUND

AT
GROUND FLOOR OF
SOLOMON'S TEMPLE,
THE WHITE AND BLACK PAVERS JOIN
TO BLEND LIGHT AND DARKNESS FOR US ALL

AN
EMBLEM OF
CALM, DIETY, AND
OVERRULING PROVIDENCE,
THE BLAZING STAR SHINES IN THE HEAVENS

ROUGH
AND PERFECT
ASHLARS IN THE EAST
EXEMPLIFY THE PROCESS
FOR SCULPTING OUR WAY TO PERFECTION

THE
MASTER WRITES
ON THE TRESTLEBOARD
THE DESIGNS BY WHICH BRETHREN
MAY CONSTRUCT THE HOUSE NOT MADE WITH HANDS

THE
CIRCUMPUNCT,
AN ASSEMBLAGE TO
HELP KEEP OUR PASSIONS IN BOUNDS,
WITH MASONS AS POINTS IN THE CIRCLE

THE
HOLY SAINTS
JOHN BORDER JOINTLY
THE CIRCUMPUNCT WITH THEIR STAFFS,
MARKING GUIDELINES OF DUTY TO GOD

AND
THE BOOK OF
CONSTITUTIONS ON
HIGH TO REMIND US OF OUR
SOLEMN MASONIC OBLIGATIONS

THE
THREE TENETS
OF OUR PROFESSION -
BROTHERLY LOVE, RELIEF, TRUTH -
HANDED DOWN FROM THOSE WHO CAME BEFORE

FOUR
CARDINAL
VIRTUES – TEMPERANCE,
FORTITUDE, PRUDENCE, JUSTICE –
THE PHILOSOPHY OF MASONRY

THE
GREATEST AND
BEST OF MEN OF ALL
AGES HAVE ENCOURAGED AND
PROMOTED OUR ART AND GENTLE CRAFT

THREE
GREAT DUTIES
NOW TO PRACTICE AND
SO INCULCATE - TO THE GREAT
ARCHITECT, YOUR NEIGHBOR, AND YOURSELF

BE
A QUIET
PEACEFUL CITIZEN,
WITH CHEERFULNESS, TRUE TO YOUR
GOVERNMENT, AND JUST TO YOUR COUNTRY

THE
INTERNAL,
NOT THE EXTERNAL,
QUALIFICATIONS OF MAN
ARE WHAT MASONRY REGARDS THE MOST

AT
YOUR LEISURE
MAY YOU IMPROVE IN
KNOWLEDGE SO AS TO CONVERSE
WITH AND TEACH AND ADVISE THE BRETHREN

KEEP
SACRED AND
INVIOLATE THE
OLD MYSTERIES OF OUR CRAFT
AS THESE DISTINGUISH YOU FROM THE REST

David Easton Potts

FELLOWCRAFT

David Easton Potts

FELLOWCRAFT DEGREE

THUS
HE SHOWED ME
AND BEHOLD THE LORD
STOOD UPON A WALL MADE BY
A PLUMB LINE WITH PLUMB LINE IN HIS HAND

THREE
WORKING TOOLS,
THE PLUMB IN THE SOUTH,
THE LEVEL IN THE WEST, AND
THE SQUARE IN THE EAST MEASURE OUR LIVES

THE
PLUMB IS USED
BY WORKING MASONS
FOR PERPENDICULARS, BUT
IT COMPELS US TO WALK UPRIGHTLY

THE
SQUARE IS USED
BY OPERATIVES
TO SQUARE WORK, BUT WE USE IT
TO SQUARE OUR ACTIONS VIRTUOUSLY

THE
LEVEL PROVES
HORIZONTALS, BUT
REMINDS THAT BLOOD IN OUR VEINS
FLOWS FROM THE SAME ALMIGHTY PARENT

WE
TRAVEL ON
THE BROAD LEVEL OF
TIME TO THAT UNDISCOVERED
COUNTRY FROM WHICH NONE OF US RETURNS

BY
OPERATIVE
MASONRY WE USE
ARCHITECTURE'S WISDOM FOR
EDIFICES IN DUE PROPORTION

BY
MASONRY
SPECULATIVE WE
BUILD PATHWAYS OF DELIGHT IN
THE GLORIOUS WORKS OF CREATION

TWO
PILLARS SHINE
BEFORE THE TEMPLE
AS GATE TO PLACES HOLY,
GUARDED BY STRENGTH AND ESTABLISHMENT

THREE
ORDERS OF
ARCHITECTURE ARE
DORIC, IONIC, AND THE
CORINTHIAN: GRAND GIFTS FROM THE GREEKS

FIVE
SENSES OF
HUMAN NATURE ARE
HEARING, SEEING, AND FEELING -
MOST REVERED - AND SMELLING AND TASTING

THE
ARTS: GRAMMAR
RHETORIC, LOGIC,
ARITHMETIC, MUSIC, AND
GEOMETRY AND ASTRONOMY

BEST
AND NOBLEST
SCIENCE IS OF OUR
EUCLID AND PYTHAGORAS:
GEOMETRY DARING GRAVITY

BY
THE POWER
OF GEOMETRY
WE OBSERVE, MARK, ORDER, AND
PERCEIVE ALL THINGS IN NATURE'S PLENTY

THE
SYMMETRY
OF NATURE'S ORDER
GAVE RISE TO SOCIETIES
AND THE BIRTH OF EVERY USEFUL ART

David Easton Potts

THE
ARCHITECT
BEGAN TO DESIGN,
AND AIDED BY TEST AND TIME,
BUILT WORKS OF AGELESS ADMIRATION

THE
LAPSE OF TIME,
THE RUTHLESS HAND OF
IGNORANCE, DEVASTATIONS
OF WAR HAVE DESTROYED OUR HISTORIES

BUT,
NONETHELESS,
FREEMASONRY STILL
SURVIVES TO PASS WISDOM ON
TO THE FOLLOWING GENERATIONS

THE
INSTRUCTIVE
TONGUES, ATTENTIVE EARS,
AND FAITHFUL BREASTS DO SAFELY
COMMUNICATE ANCIENT MYSTERIES

OUR
SACRED AND
SYMBOLIC EMBLEMS
IMPRINT ON THE MIND WISE AND
SERIOUS TRUTHS FOR ALL TO DISCERN

SUCH
THE NATURE
IS OF YOUR NEWLY
FOUND DUTIES OF FELLOWCRAFT,
AND TO THESE COMMITMENTS YOU ARE BOUND

David Easton Potts

MASTER MASON

MASTER MASON DEGREE

THE
LODGE OPENS
IN DUE AND ANCIENT
FORM AND IN ONE ACCORD, BOUND
TOGETHER IN DUTY AND RESPECT

WE
BESEECH THEE
O LORD TO BLESS OUR
PRESENT ASSEMBLAGE AND TO
ILLUMINATE OUR MINDS WITH WISDOM

MAY
THIS MEETING,
BEGUN IN ORDER,
BE CONDUCTED IN PEACE AND
CLOSED IN HARMONY - SO MOTE IT BE

AND
REMEMBER
NOW THY CREATOR
IN THE DAYS OF THY YOUTH, WHILE
THE EVIL DAYS NOR THE YEARS DRAW NIGH

THEN
SHALL THE DUST
RETURN TO THE EARTH
AS IT WAS AND THE SPIRIT
SHALL RETURN UNTO GOD WHO GAVE IT

OF
A MASTER
MASON ARE ALL THE
IMPLEMENTS OF MASONRY,
MORE ESPECIALLY THE TROWEL

THE
TROWEL IS
USED TO SPREAD CEMENT
BY OPERATIVES, BUT WE
IN SYMBOL OF OUR BROTHERLY LOVE

A
TEMPLE OF
LIVING STONES, AMONG
WHOM NO CONTENTION SHOULD BE
ALLOWED, SAVE WHO BEST WORKS AND AGREES

THOU
GOD KNOWEST
OUR DOWNSITTING AND
UPRISING, UNDERSTANDEST
OUR THOUGHTS AFAR OFF - HEAR OUR PRAYER

SHIELD
AND DEFEND
US FROM THE EVIL
INTENTS OF OUR ENEMIES,
SUPPORT US IN TRIALS, AFFLICTIONS

AND
O LORD, HAVE
COMPASSION ON THE
CHILDREN OF THY CREATION;
SAVE THEM WITH ETERNAL SALVATION

IT
HAS BEEN THE
PRACTICE OF AGES
TO ERECT MONUMENTS TO
THE MEMORY OF EXALTED WORTH

THE
VIRGIN WEEPS
OVER THE BROKEN
COLUMN WITH URN IN ONE HAND
AND EVERGREEN SPRIG IN THE OTHER

THE
WISDOM OF
KING SOLOMON, THE
STRENGTH OF KING HIRAM, AND THE
SKILL AND TALENT OF HIRAM ABIFF

ON
MORIAH
WHERE ABRAHAM DID
OFFER UP HIS SON ISAAC,
KING SOLOMON SO BUILT HIS TEMPLE

MORE
THAN SEVEN
YEARS IT NEITHER RAINED
IN DAYTIME, NOR SOUND OF AXE,
HAMMER, OR ANY IRON TOOL WAS HEARD

THE
THREE STAGES
OF HUMAN LIFE ARE
YOUTH AND MANHOOD AND OLD AGE -
AS THE THREE DEGREES OF MASONRY

AN
EMBLEM OF
A PURE HEART, THE POT
OF INCENSE RADIATES AND
WARMS OUR SOULS IN GRATITUDE FOR LIFE

THE
BEEHIVE IS
EMBLEMATIC OF
MAN'S INDUSTRY AND REMINDS
US THAT WE WERE FORMED FOR ACTIVE LIFE

THE
BOOK OF OUR
CONSTITUTIONS TYLED
BY THE SWORD DOTH WARN US TO
BE EVER WATCHFUL IN WORDS AND DEEDS

A
SWORD POINTING
TO A NAKED HEART
DEMONSTRATES THAT JUSTICE WILL
SOONER OR LATER OVERTAKE US

ALL
SEEING EYE
WITH RAYS DESCENDING,
THE GREAT ARCHITECT OBSERVES
US ALL WITH HIS WATCHFUL CARE AND LOVE

SUN
MOON AND STARS
PERVADE THE INMOST
RECESSES OF HUMAN HEARTS
AND MINDS, LINKING US TO SACRED TIME

ARK
AND ANCHOR
SAFELY CARRY US
OVER TROUBLED WATERS AND
FIRMLY MOOR US IN PEACEFUL HARBORS

AN
INVENTION
OF PYTHAGORAS,
FRIEND AND BROTHER, IS THE PURE
FORTY-SEVENTH PROBLEM OF EUCLID

THE
HOURGLASS IS
EMBLEMATIC OF
HUMAN LIFE. YOU CAN'T HOLD BACK
THE SANDS OF TIME, SO LIVE WITH PURPOSE

THE
SCYTHE OF TIME
CUTS THE THREAD OF LIFE,
SENDING US TO THE PLACE WHERE
BEFORE US OUR FATHERS HAVE JOURNEYED

THE
SETTING MAUL,
SPADE, COFFIN, AND A
SPRIG OF ACACIA FORCE THOUGHTS
OF DEATH, RENEWAL, AND LIFE BEYOND

AND
SOLEMN STRIKES
THE FUNERAL CHIME.
WAFT OUR FRIEND AND BROTHER HOME.
LORD ABOVE FILL HEARTS WITH TRUTH AND LOVE

FIVE
FELLOWSHIP
POINTS UPON THE STAR,
ALL LINES AND ANGLES EQUAL,
BOUNDED BY SACRED GEOMETRY

LET
US FOLLOW
GRAND MASTER HIRAM
ABIFF'S STEADFAST PIETY
AND INFLEXIBLE FIDELITY

YOU
ARE NOW A
FREE AND ACCEPTED
MASON, AND AS SUCH ARE BOUND
TO OBEY THE TENETS OF OUR CRAFT

LET
NO MOTIVE
MAKE YOU SWERVE FROM YOUR
DUTY, VIOLATE YOUR VOWS,
OR BETRAY YOUR TRUST – BE FIRM AND TRUE

David Easton Potts

HEAR
OUR HUMBLE
THANKS FOR ALL MERCIES
GIVEN, AND ESPECIALLY
FOR THIS FRIENDLY AND SOCIAL MEETING

MAY
WE ALL OF
US DAILY INCREASE
IN FAITH, HOPE AND CHARITY,
MORE SO IN THE BOND OF CHARITY

MAY
THE BLESSING
OF HEAVEN REST ON
US AND MAY BROTHERLY LOVE
PREVAIL AND MORAL VIRTUE GUIDE US

WE
ARE NOW TO
QUIT THIS RETREAT TO
MIX AGAIN WITH THE WORLD, NOT
FORGETTING THE DUTIES WE HAVE LEARNED

WE'VE
SOLEMNLY
BOUND OURSELVES TO AID,
HELP, AND COUNSEL EACH BROTHER
WHO SHALL NEED RELIEF AND ASSISTANCE

THESE
GENEROUS
PRINCIPLES ARE TO
EXTEND TO EVERYONE.
DO GOOD UNTO ALL AND FAITHFUL BE

MARK MASTER

MARK MASTER DEGREE

EVE
OF WEEK'S SIXTH
DAY THE FELLOWCRAFTS
MEET IN THE MIDDLE CHAMBER
TO RECEIVE WAGES FOR THEIR LABOR

THE
CRAFTSMEN FROM
THE QUARRIES COME WITH
ALL THEIR WORK FOR INSPECTION.
THEY MARKED THEIR PIECES ACCORDINGLY

THE
OVERSEERS
HAVE STRICT ORDERS TO
INSPECT AND PASS ONLY THOSE
STONES THAT ARE SQUARE WORK FOR THE TEMPLE

BY
THE CHISEL'S
EDGE THE MASON CLEAVES
THE STONE WITH HIS MARK TO SHOW
THE WORK TO BE HIS AND HIS ALONE

SHOULD
THEY LABOR
IN THE QUARRIES AND
EXHIBIT A SPECIMEN
OF ARTFUL SKILL, THEN THEY MAY PASS ON

IF
THEIR LABORS
ARE APPROVED, THEN THEY
ARE TAUGHT TO RECEIVE WAGES
IN THE PROPER MANNER FOR MASONS

ONE
SHOULD NEVER
IMPOSE UPON THE
CRAFT AND EXPECT TO RECEIVE
WAGES WHEN THERE ARE NO WAGES DUE

THEN
HE BROUGHT ME
BACK TOWARD THE WAY
OF THE GATE OF THE OUTWARD
SANCTUARY WHICH LOOKED TO THE EAST

SON
OF MAN MARK
WELL AND BEHOLD WITH
THINE EYES AND HEAR WITH THINE EARS
ALL THAT I SAY TO THEE OF THE LAWS

David Easton Potts

A
BROTHER MARK
MASTER MUST NEVER
REJECT A BROTHER'S APPEAL
FOR HELP WHEN GIVING HIS MASON'S MARK

WE
ARE TOO APT,
MY BROTHER, WHEN PLEAS
OF CHARITY COME TO US
TO TURN ASIDE SAYING WE HAVE NAUGHT

IF
WE DO NOT
AID HIM THEN WE MUST
RETURN HIS MARK WITH THE PRICE
OF ONE-HALF SHEKEL - ONE-FOURTH DOLLAR

THE
ONE GIVING
THE MARK AND ASKING
RELIEF IS HIRAM ABIFF,
A POOR MAN BUT FOR HIS GREAT TALENT

THE
ONE GIVING
BACK THE MARK GRANTING
SUPPORT IS KING SOLOMON,
A RICH MAN NOTED FOR HIS KINDNESS

THE
KEYSTONE WAS
WROUGHT BY GRAND MASTER
HIRAM ABIFF FOR ONE OF
KING SOLOMON'S PRINCIPAL ARCHES

THE
STONE WHICH THE
BUILDERS REJECTED
IS BECOME THE HEAD OF THE
CORNER AND THIS WAS THE LORD'S DOING

TO
THE MAN THAT
OVERCOMETH WILL
I GIVE HIM A WHITE STONE AND
IN IT A NEW NAME SHALL BE WRITTEN

THE
CHISEL STANDS
FOR EDUCATION.
IT REMOVES THE ROUGHNESS OF
THE MIND TO REVEAL INNER WISDOM

THE
MALLET IS
TO REDUCE MAN TO
A PROPER LEVEL SO THAT
HE CAN LEARN TO BE CONTENT IN LIFE

YOU
WHO HAVE PASSED
THE SQUARE MARCH FORWARD
WITH YOUR MARK IN VIEW AND SO
CLAIM YOUR WAGES WITH THE JUST AND TRUE

IF
A WORKER
AGREES TO WAGES
OF A PENNY A DAY, THEN
THE WORKER SHOULD REMAIN SATISFIED

DO
REMEMBER,
THE LAST SHALL BE FIRST,
AND THE FIRST SHALL BE LAST; FOR
MANY BE CALLED, BUT FEW ARE CHOSEN

LET
YOUR CONDUCT
AMONG YOUR BRETHREN
BE SUCH AS MAY STAND THE TEST
AND CHECK OF THE GRAND OVERSEER'S SQUARE

SO
YOU MAYN'T BE
LIKE THE UNFINISHED,
IMPERFECT WORKINGS OF THE
NEGLIGENT AND UNFAITHFUL OF OLD

THUS
REMEMBER,
THE STONE THE BUILDERS
REJECTED, WITH WORTH UNKNOWN,
BECAME THE CHIEF STONE OF THE CORNER

AND
MAY YOU HAVE
SURENESS THAT AMONG
ALL MARK MASTER MASONS YOU
WILL FIND GUIDANCE FROM FRIENDS AND BROTHERS

NOW
TO OUR PRAISE
OF THOSE WHO TRIUMPHED
O'ER THE FOES OF MASON'S ART.
MAY ALL THEIR VIRTUES BE IN OUR HEARTS

David Easton Potts

SELECT AND ROYAL MASTERS

SELECT MASTERS DEGREE

HIS
FOUNDATION
IS IN THE HOLY
MOUNTAINS. GLORIOUS THINGS ARE
SPOKEN OF THEE, O CITY OF GOD

OF
ZION IT
SHALL BE SAID, THIS AND
THAT MAN WAS BORN IN HER; THE
HIGHEST HIMSELF SHALL ESTABLISH HER

THE
SELECT ONES
ARE FOUND ALL TO BE
PRESENT, THE GUARDS ARE ORDERED
SET, AND ALL IS SECURE AND SECRET

OUR
FIRST THREE GRAND
MASTERS VOWED NOT TO
CONFER THE MASTER'S DEGREE
UNTIL THE TEMPLE WAS COMPLETED,

THEY
AGREEING,
AND THEN ONLY TO
THOSE WHO PROVED THEMSELVES WORTHY
OF SKILL, VIRTUE, AND FIDELITY

FROM
WISDOM AND
KNOWLEDGE OF SCRIPTURES
THE THREE KNEW THE TEMPLE WOULD
BE DESTROYED AND SACRED KNOWLEDGE LOST

THEY
CONSTRUCTED
IN SECRECY A
VAULT BENEATH THE TEMPLE TO
PRESERVE ALL THE SACRED ARTICLES

TO
WORK IN THE
VAULT WERE SELECTED
MEN FROM GEBAL, A CITY
IN PHOENICIA, A PLACE OF CRAFTSMEN

A
PARTICULAR
FRIEND OF SOLOMON,
BY NAME ZABUD, LEARNED
THAT SECRET WORK WAS GOING
ON AND ASKED THE KING FOR AN ANSWER

KING
SOLOMON
TOLD ZABUD TO BE
CONTENT AND THE TIME WOULD COME
WHEN THE VAULT WOULD BE OPEN TO HIM

BUT
ONE EVENING,
WHEN ZABUD WAS IN
SEARCH OF THE KING, FOUND THE VAULT
DOOR WIDE OPEN AND NOT ATTENDED

HE
TOOK IT FOR
GRANTED THAT THE DOOR
HAD BEEN LEFT OPEN FOR HIM
AGREEABLE TO THE KING'S PROMISE

BUT
THE CAPTAIN
OF THE GUARD CHALLENGED
ZABUD DEMANDING PROOF OF
RIGHT OF ENTRANCE, WHICH HE COULD NOT GIVE

THEN
ZABUD WAS
SEIZED AND BOUND AS AN
INTRUDER AND SOLOMON
WAS CALLED IN RESPONSE TO THE ALARM

THE
INTRUDER
WAS ORDERED PUT TO
DEATH AT ONCE, BUT THEN ZABUD
WAS RECOGNIZED BY KING SOLOMON

KING
SOLOMON
CONFERRED WITH HIS FRIEND
KING HIRAM OF TYRE AND GRAND
MASTER HIRAM ABIFF FOR ADVICE

KING
HIRAM SAID
THE NUMBER OF MEN
FOR THE VAULT WAS ALREADY
AGREED AND NO MORE COULD BE ADDED

BUT
GRAND MASTER
HIRAM ABIFF GAVE
THE OBSERVATION THAT HE
COULD REPLACE THE GUARD WHO WAS SLEEPING

THEN
ZABUD WAS
PARDONED FOR HIS ZEAL
AND FERVENCY, MISTAKEN
FOR PRYING AND DISOBEDIENCE

THUS
THE THREE GRAND
MASTERS ADMITTED
ZABUD TO THE VAULT BELOW
THE TEMPLE GUARDING SACRED ITEMS

BE
SENSIBLE
THAT OBLIGATIONS
ARE INCREASED IN PROPORTION
TO YOUR PRIVILEGES IN YOUR LIFE

LET
IT BE YOUR
CONTINUAL CARE
TO PROVE YOURSELF WORTHY OF
THE CONFIDENCE NOW REPOSED IN YOU

LET
UPRIGHTNESS
AND INTEGRITY
ATTEND YOUR STEPS. LET JUSTICE
AND MERCY ALWAYS MARK YOUR CONDUCT

LET
FERVENCY
AND ZEAL STIMULATE
YOU IN THE DISCHARGE OF THE
MANY DUTIES INCUMBENT ON YOU

BUT
SUFFER NOT
AN IMPERTINENT
CURIOSITY TO LEAD
YOURSELF ASTRAY OR INTO DANGER

BE
DEAF TO ALL
INSINUATIONS
WHICH WEAKEN YOUR RESOLVE OR
TEMPT YOU INTO DISOBEDIENCE

LET
SILENCE AND
SECRECY – HALLOWED
VIRTUES OF SELECT MASTERS –
AT ALL TIMES BE CAREFULLY OBSERVED

ROYAL MASTERS DEGREE

AND
HE SET THE
CHERUBIM WITHIN
THE INNER HOUSE AND THEY STRETCHED
FORTH SO THE WING OF ONE TOUCHED ONE WALL,

AND
THE WING OF
THE OTHER TOUCHED THE
OTHER WALL, AND THEIR WINGS IN
THE MID OF THE HOUSE TOUCHED EACH OTHER

THE
ARK, GLORY
OF ISRAEL, WAS
SEATED IN THE HOLY PLACE
UNDER THE WINGS OF THE CHERUBIM

David Easton Potts

IN
THE SANCTUM
SANCTORUM ON THE
EVENING BEFORE HIS DEATH
WAS OUR GRAND MASTER HIRAM ABIFF

AS
PRINCIPAL
ARCHITECT OF THE
TEMPLE HE WAS IN CHARGE OF
FINISHING THE SANCTUM SANCTORUM,

AND
ASSISTED
BY SEVEN EXPERT
FELLOWCRAFTS SELECTED BY
KING SOLOMON FOR THOSE PURPOSES

ONE
FELLOWCRAFT,
ADONIRAM, WAS
THE HEAD OF THESE MEN SKILLED IN
THE ARTS AND SCIENCES AND SCULPTURE

AND
IT IS SAID
WAS THE PRINCIPAL
CONSPIRATOR TO EXTORT
THE SECRET WORD FROM HIRAM ABIFF

ON
ACCOUNT OF
THIS CONVERSATION,
HE RECANTED AND CONVINCED
ELEVEN OTHERS TO DO THE SAME

IT
WAS ON THE
EVE OF THE SIXTH DAY
WHEN ALL THE HOLY VESSELS
WERE BROUGHT TO THE SANCTUM SANCTORUM,

AND
INSPECTED.
THE CRAFT HAD WITHDRAWN
THEREFROM WHEN ADONIRAM
APPROACHED GRAND MASTER HIRAM ABIFF

WHEN
SHALL WE GET
THE MASTER'S DEGREE?
HIRAM, WHO FREQUENTLY HAD
BEEN ASKED THIS QUESTION RESPONDED THUS:

WHEN
THE TEMPLE
IS COMPLETE, THE THREE
GRAND MASTERS PRESENT AND IN
AGREEMENT, AND YOU ARE FOUND WORTHY

NOT
SATISFIED,
ADONIRAM ASKED:
SUPPOSE YOU DIED, HOW THEN SHALL
WE ALL RECEIVE THE MASTER'S DEGREE?

STRUCK
BY THOSE WORDS
AND REFLECTING ON
LIFE'S UNCERTAINTY, HIRAM
REPLIED: "WHEN I DIE BURY IT HERE"

David Easton Potts

MOST EXCELLENT MASTER

MOST EXCELLENT MASTER DEGREE

WHO
SHALL ASCEND
INTO THE HILL OF
THE LORD? HE WITH CLEAN HANDS, A
PURE HEART, AND NO VANITY IN SOUL

LIFT
UP YOUR HEADS,
O YE GATES, AND BE
YE LIFT UP, EVERLASTING
DOORS, THE KING OF GLORY SHALL COME IN

WHEN
THE TEMPLE
WAS COMPLETED A
DAY WAS SET APART FOR ITS
DEDICATION AND CEREMONY

KING
SOLOMON,
PASSING THROUGHOUT ITS
SEVERAL APARTMENTS, FOUND
IT TO BE PERFECT IN ALL ITS PARTS

THE
WHOLE TEMPLE
SHINED, GLOWED, AND DAZZLED
THE EYES OF SUCH AS ENTERED
BY THE SPLENDOR OF GOLD ALL AROUND

ALL
HAIL TO THE
MORNING THAT BIDS US
REJOICE, THE TEMPLE IS NOW
COMPLETED, THEN EXALT HIGH EACH VOICE

THE
CAPSTONE IS
NOW FINISHED AND OUR
LABOR IS OVER, THE SOUND
OF THE GAVEL SHALL HAIL US NO MORE

SO
COMPANIONS
ASSEMBLE ON THIS
JOYFUL DAY, THE OCCASION
IS GLORIOUS, THE KEYSTONE TO LAY

THE
PROMISE IS
FULFILLED BY ANCIENT
OF DAYS. BRING FORTH THE CAPSTONE
WITH SHOUTING AND PRAISE, SHOUTING AND PRAISE

THERE
IS NO MORE
NEED FOR LEVEL OR
PLUMB LINE, AND THE TROWEL AND
GAVEL, AND THE COMPASS, AND THE SQUARE

OUR
WORKS ARE NOW
COMPLETED AND THE
ARK IS SAFELY SEATED. WE
SHALL BE GREETED AS WORKMEN MOST RARE

WE
ACCEPT AND
RECEIVE THEM, THE MOST
EXCELLENT MASTERS, WITH THEIR
MASONS' KNOWLEDGE TO SPREAD FAR AND WIDE

THEN
SOLOMON
SAID, "THE LORD HATH SAID
THAT HE WOULD DWELL IN DARKNESS,
BUT I HAVE BUILT A HOUSE FOREVER"

WHEN
SOLOMON
ENDED HIS PRAYERS
THE FIRE CAME DOWN FROM HEAVEN.
THE GLORY OF THE LORD FILLED THE HOUSE

FOR
HE IS GOOD,
HIS MERCY ENDURES
FOREVER, FOR HE IS GOOD,
HIS MERCY ENDURETH FOREVER

WHEN
THE TEMPLE
WAS COMPLETED THE
CRAFTSMEN WERE PERMITTED TO
TRAVEL AND RECEIVE MASTER'S WAGES

KING
SOLOMON
KEPT MOST EXCELLENT
MASTERS FOR THE NEW TEMPLE
AND ORGANIZED THEM INTO A LODGE

YOUR
ADMITTANCE
TO THIS DEGREE OF
MASONRY IS PROOF OF THE
GOOD OPINION OF THE LODGE BRETHREN

LET
THIS INDUCE
YOU TO BE CAREFUL
OF MISCONDUCT AND LACK OF
ATTENTION FORFEITING THEIR ESTEEM

IT
IS ONE OF
YOUR DUTIES AS A
MOST EXCELLENT MASTER TO
DISPENSE LIGHT TO THE UNTAUGHT MASON

LET
IT THEREFORE
BE YOUR INCESSANT
TASK TO ACQUIRE SUCH KNOWLEDGE
TO PRESERVE THIS TITLE NOW CONFERRED

David Easton Potts

ROYAL ARCH

ROYAL ARCH DEGREE

MAY
HOLINESS
TO THE LORD BE SO
ENGRAVEN UPON ALL OF
OUR FUTURE THOUGHTS, WORDS, DEEDS, AND ACTIONS

MAY
WE DAILY
SEARCH FOR THE TRUTH. MAY
WE SHARE THE PURITY OF
THOSE WHO HEAR AND KEEP THE SACRED WORD

SO
NOW BRETHREN,
IN PURSUING YOUR
INTENTIONS, YOU WILL TRAVEL
ROUGH AND RUGGED PATHS AS THOSE BEFORE

AND
MOSES LED
THE FLOCK OF JETHRO
TO THE BACK OF THE DESERT
AND ARRIVED AT THE MOUNTAIN OF GOD

AND
THE ANGEL
OF THE LORD APPEARED
UNTO HIM IN A FLAME OF
FIRE OUT OF THE MIDDLE OF A BUSH

AND
WHEN THE LORD
SAW THAT HE TURNED TO
SEE, HE CALLED UNTO HIM FROM
THE BUSH AND MOSES SAID, "HERE AM I"

AND
GOD SAID, DRAW
NOT NIGH, PUT OFF THY
SHOES FROM THY FEET FOR THE PLACE
WHEREON THOU STANDEST IS HOLY GROUND

I
AM THE GOD
OF THY FATHER, THE
GOD OF ABRAHAM, ISAAC,
JACOB. MOSES HID HIS FACE FROM GOD

BUT
THE PRIESTS AND
PEOPLE POLLUTED
THE HOUSE OF THE LORD, WHICH HE
HAD THUS ALLOWED IN JERUSALEM

AND
GOD SENT TO
THEM HIS MESSENGERS
BECAUSE HE HAD COMPASSION
ON HIS PEOPLE AND HIS DWELLING SPACE

BUT
THEY MOCKED THE
MESSENGERS OF GOD
UNTIL THE LORD'S WRATH AROSE
ON HIS PEOPLE WITHOUT REMEDY

GOD
BROUGHT UPON
THEM THE KING OF THE
CHALDEES WHO SLEW THEIR YOUNG MEN
IN THE HOUSE OF THEIR SANCTUARY

ALL
THE VESSELS
OF THE HOUSE OF GOD,
THE TREASURES, AND THE REST OF
THE PEOPLE HE BROUGHT TO BABYLON,

WHERE
THEY BECAME
SERVANTS TO HIM AND
HIS SONS UNTIL THE TIME OF
THE REIGN OF THE KINGDOM OF PERSIA

NOW
COMPANIONS,
YOU REPRESENT THREE
OF OUR BRETHREN IN THE TIME
OF BABYLONISH CAPTIVITY

THUS,
ACCORDING
TO A PROPHECY,
WHEN CYRUS ASCENDS TO THE
PERSIAN THRONE YOU'LL BE LIBERATED

HIS
GOD BE WITH
HIM AND LET HIM GO
UP TO JERUSALEM IN
JUDAH AND BUILD THE HOUSE OF THE LORD

WE
ARE WILLING
TO GO UP BUT ARE
DOUBTFUL OF THE RECEPTION
AT THE HANDS OF OUR ANCIENT BRETHREN

YOU
SHALL SAY TO
THEM THE GOD OF YOUR
FATHERS HAS SENT US UNTO
YOU TO HELP BUILD THE HOUSE OF THE LORD

THIS
IS A ROUGH
ROAD, BUT WHAT IS THIS?
AN ALTAR LEFT UNINJURED.
LET US NOW KNEEL AND PRAY BEFORE IT

IN
THEE IS MY
TRUST. LEAVE NOT MY SOUL
DESTITUTE. AND SO KEEP ME
FROM THE SNARES WHICH THEY HAVE LAID FOR ME

I
WILL BRING THE
BLIND BY A WAY THEY
KNEW NOT. I WILL LEAD THEM IN
PATHS UNKNOWN AND MAKE CROOKED THINGS
STRAIGHT

I
ALSO WILL
MAKE THE DARKNESS LIGHT
BEFORE THEM. THESE THINGS WILL I
DO UNTO THEM AND NOT FORSAKE THEM

WHEN
MY SPIRIT
WAS OVERWHELMED ALL
WITHIN ME, THEN THOU KNEWEST
MY PATH IN THE WAY WHEREIN I WALKED

I
LOOKED ON MY
RIGHT HAND AND BEHELD
BUT THERE WAS NO MAN THAT WOULD
KNOW ME AND NO MAN CARED FOR MY SOUL

I
CRIED UNTO
THEE, O LORD. THOU ART
MY REFUGE. BRING MY SOUL OUT
OF DARKNESS THAT I MAY PRAISE THY NAME

NOW
I SEE THE
NOBLE MOUNTAINS WHERE
HEWERS OF ADONIRAM
PREPARED THE TIMBERS FOR THE TEMPLE

OH!
GLORIOUS
ASSOCIATIONS.
SUCH GODLIKE SCENERY AND
GODLIKE MEN FOR GODLIKE PURPOSES

HEAR
ME O LORD
MY SPIRIT FAILS, HIDE
NOT MY FACE FROM THEE LEST I
BE LIKE THEM THAT GO DOWN IN THE PIT

OH!
THERE IT IS.
JERUSALEM CAN
NOW BE SEEN GLORIOUSLY
SLEEPING IN THE EVENING SUNLIGHT

MOUNT
MORIAH'S
SUMMIT, UP FROM THE
POOL OF SILOAM, WHERE LAY
FRAGMENTS OF OUR GLORIOUS TEMPLE

ALL
SCATTERED IN
DUST ARE THE MIGHTY
WORKS OF SOLOMON AND THE
MATCHLESS CONCEPTS OF HIRAM ABIFF

IF
I FORGET
THEE JERUSALEM
AND PREFER THEE NOT THEN MAY
MY TONGUE CLEAVE TO THE ROOF OF MY MOUTH

LET
US REPAIR
THITHER AND OFFER
OUR HUMBLE SERVICES TO
ASSIST IN THE TEMPLE'S REBUILDING

WHO
ARE YOU? WE
ARE OF YOUR KINDRED
SPRUNG FROM NOBLE GIBLIMITES
WHO WROUGHT HARD TO BUILD THE FIRST TEMPLE

IN
PROCEEDING
FURTHER, YOU MUST NOW
PASS THE FIRST VEIL. HOW DO YOU
EXPECT TO GAIN ADMITTANCE THROUGH IT?

BY
BENEFIT
OF THE REGULAR
PASS WE RECEIVED AT THE START
OF OUR LONG JOURNEY FROM BABYLON

YOUR
REGULAR
PASS IS RIGHT. YOU ALL
ARE MOST EXCELLENT MASTERS,
OR THUS FAR YOU COULD NOT HAVE HERE COME

BUT
FURTHER YOU
CANNOT GO WITHOUT
MY WORDS, SIGNS, AND THE WORDS OF
EXHORTATION, WHICH I NOW GIVE YOU

YOU
HAVE PASSED THE
VEILS. NOW YOU MUST SHOW
THE GRAND COUNCIL WILLINGNESS
FOR EVEN THE MOST SERVILE LABOR

WE'RE
ASSURED YOU
ARE MOST EXCELLENT
MASTERS AND WILLING TO DO
ANY LABOR IN THIS REBUILDING

BUT
AT PRESENT
THE RUBBISH MUST BE
REMOVED FROM THE OLD TEMPLE
BEFORE LAYING THE NEW FOUNDATION

YOU
WILL PRESERVE
EVERYTHING YOU
FIND OF IMPORTANCE TO THE
CRAFT AND PASS IT TO THE GRAND COUNCIL

MOST
EXCELLENT
HIGH PRIEST, KING AND SCRIBE,
WE REPAIRED TO THE RUBBISH,
DESCENDED, AND FOUND THESE ARTICLES

MY
COMPANIONS,
THESE ARE IMPORTANT
AND HAVE GREAT MEANING FOR US.
THEY HAVE BEEN BURIED FOR MANY YEARS

YOU
SOON WILL BE
EXALTED AS NEW
ROYAL ARCH MASONS, THE MOST
SUBLIME DEGREE OF ALL PRECEDING

IT
BRINGS TO LIGHT
THOSE VALUABLE
SECRETS AND ALL KNOWLEDGE WHICH
COMPLETE THE MASONIC CHARACTER

THE
TOOLS OF THE
ROYAL ARCH MASON,
IN ADDITION TO THOSE IN
YOUR HANDS, ARE THE SQUARE AND COMPASSES

THE
TRIANGLE
EQUILATERAL
ON WHICH THE OMNIFICENT
WORD WAS FOUND IS EMBLEMATIC OF

THREE
ATTRIBUTES
OF DEITY. THUS:
OMNISCIENCE, OMNIPOTENCE,
AND EVERLASTING OMNIPRESENCE

ALL
THREE EQUAL
ANGLES CONSTITUTE
BUT ONE TRIANGLE, MEANING
THAT ALL THREE REPRESENT BUT ONE GOD

.

David Easton Potts

A
PURE CIRCLE
ENCOMPASSES THE
TRIANGLE OF DIETY,
WITHOUT DAYS BEGINNING OR TIME'S END

YOU'VE
ASCENDED
BY UNVARYING
GRADATION OF YOUR JOURNEY
TO THE PEAK OF ANCIENT MASONRY

YOU
HAVE REACHED THE
SANCTUM SANCTORUM
AND WITH FAITHFUL FEW HAVE BEEN
ADMITTED INTO THE SECRET VAULT

YOU
HAVE LEARNED HOW
THE OMNIFICENT
WORD WAS PRESERVED THROUGH THE WISE
ADVICE OF THE WIDOW'S SON OF TYRE

YOU
HAVE SEEN THE
SACRED TREASURES OF
THE FORMER TEMPLE BROUGHT TO
LIGHT, THE BLESSED BOOK RESTORED TO PLACE

YOU
HAVE ENTERED
INTO THE SPIRIT
OF THESE SOLEMN RITES AND LEARNED
THE FULL IMPORT OF OUR CRAFT'S SYMBOLS

ALL
THE DEGREES
YOU'VE HAD BEFORE HAVE
LED YOU TO THIS MOMENT AND
POINT OF RECEPTION WITHIN THE VEILS

THE
MYSTERIES
AND RITES DEVELOPED
IN THIS DEGREE ARE UNCHANGED
BY TIME, UNCONTROLLED BY PREJUDICE

WE
EXPECT AND
TRUST YOU WILL REGARD
THEM WITH YOUR VENERATION
AND TRANSMIT THEM TO YOUR SUCCESSORS

NOW
COMPANIONS,
ALTHOUGH YOU'VE RECEIVED
INSTRUCTION IN OUR NOBLE
CRAFT YOUR LABORS ARE NOT YET ENDED

SHOULD
GOD IN HIS
ALL-WISE PROVIDENCE
EXTEND YOUR LENGTH OF DAYS, SPEND
THEM IN HIS SERVICE AND TO OUR CRAFT

AND
LIKE THE LEAF
THAT FALLS TO NOURISH
ROOTS, RENDER YOUR DECLINING
YEARS BENEFICIAL TO ALL MANKIND

IN
ALL AGES
SOME MEN HAVE SOUGHT TO
ERECT MONUMENTS TO THEIR
OWN GREATNESS, BUT AS YET ALL IN VAIN

THEY
HAVE DAUBED WITH
UNTEMPERED MORTAR
AND ADMITTED INTO THEIR
STRUCTURES HARMFUL PRIDE AND AMBITION

HENCE
THEIR TREASURED
EDIFICES HAVE
TOPPLED FROM THEIR BASES OR
BEEN TORN BY INTERNAL VIOLENCE

AND
WHERE ARE THEY
NOW? THE WEEPING VOICE
OF HISTORY ANSWERS WITH
"FALLEN", SUNK BENEATH THE HORIZON

BUT
THE PROUD AND
LOFTY STRUCTURE OF
OUR ANCIENT CRAFT, SUPPORTED
AND SUSTAINED BY THE GREAT HIGH PRIEST, WILL

STAND
UNTIL THE
SUN SHALL CEASE TO RISE
AND GILD ITS TOWERS OR THE
MOON LIGHT ITS STARRY DECKED CANOPY

David Easton Potts

EPILOGUE

BY
THE WISDOM
OF THE SUPREME HIGH
PRIEST MAY WE BE DIRECTED,
BY HIS STRENGTH MAY WE BE ENABLED,

BY
THE BEAUTY
OF HIS HOLINESS
MAY WE BE INCITED TO
KEEP OBLIGATIONS ENJOINED ON US,

THE
MYSTERIES
UNFOLDED TO US,
AND PRACTICE ALL DUTIES OUT
OF CHAPTER THAT ARE INSTILLED IN IT

About the Author

David Easton Potts is a Past Master of Cherrydale-Columbia Lodge No. 42 in Arlington Virginia, Past District Deputy Grand Master of Virginia District 1A, Past High Priest of Arlington Royal Arch Chapter No. 35, Past Commander member of Old Dominion Commandery No. 11 in Alexandria, and Past Sovereign Master of Lord Fairfax Council No. 90, Allied Masonic Degrees. He is a member of Kemper-Macon Ware Lodge No. 64 in Falls Church, the Valley of Alexandria Scottish Rite, Washington & Lee York Rite College No. 93, Rose of Sharon Priory No. 2 (KYCH), Virginia Council No. 12 Knight Masons, and Nova Vita Tabernacle No. 73 Holy Royal Arch Knight Templar Priests.

David is a retired U.S. Air Force colonel who served in a variety of posts, including assignments to the U.S. Embassy in Moscow and the U.S. Embassy in Prague. Following his military service, he worked in military aircraft business development for the Lockheed Martin Aeronautics Company in Fort Worth, Texas, and then for Corporate Strategy and Business Development at Lockheed Martin's Headquarters in Bethesda, Maryland. He has a bachelor's degree in Communications from Texas Christian University, a master's degree in National Security Affairs from the Naval Postgraduate School, and a Doctor of Philosophy in Russian Studies from Georgetown University.